This Is Me, Full Stop.

Philip Cowell and Caz Hildebrand

This Is Me, Full Stop.

PARTICULAR
BOOKS

PARTICULAR BOOKS

UK | USA | Canada | Ireland | Australia
India | New Zealand | South Africa

Particular Books is part of the Penguin Random House group of companies
whose addresses can be found at global.penguinrandomhouse.com.

Penguin
Random House
UK

First published 2017
001

Copyright © Inkipit, 2017
The moral rights of the authors have been asserted

Printed in Italy by L.E.G.O S.p.A.

A CIP catalogue record for this book is available
from the British Library

ISBN: 978-1-846-14936-8

Idea & Words: Philip Cowell
Design & Illustration: Caz Hildebrand

. , ; : ( ) – " " " " / ! ? ...

. , ; : ( ) – " " " " / ! ? ...

. , ; : ( ) – " " " " / ! ? ...

. , ; : ( ) – " " " " / ! ? ...

. , ; : ( ) – " " " " / ! ? ...

This is me, full stop.

Look, this is me, far away.

And this is me, up close.

This is me, in 3D.

I've ended sentences for centuries.

In Ancient Greece, I was placed above the line.

I fully stop so you can start.

I'm really good at endings.

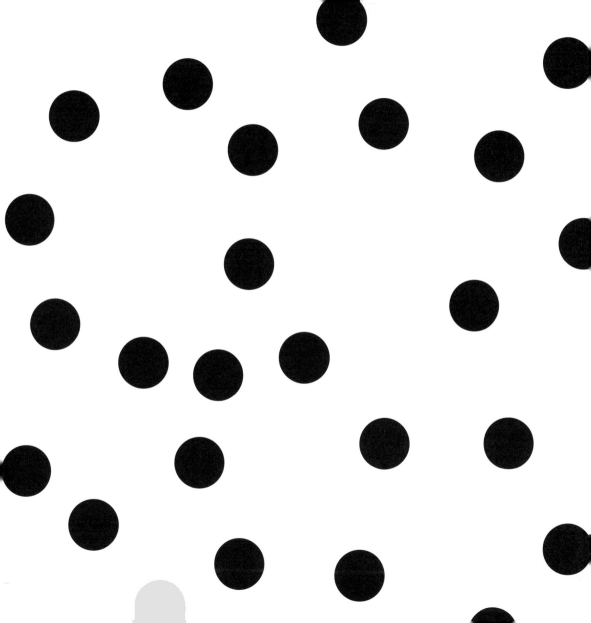

This is me, comma.

I'm a full stop in a wind machine.

I'm all about pace, flow, tempo.

Perfectly placed, I give your sentences a bit of a breather.

Keep it up, keep it up!

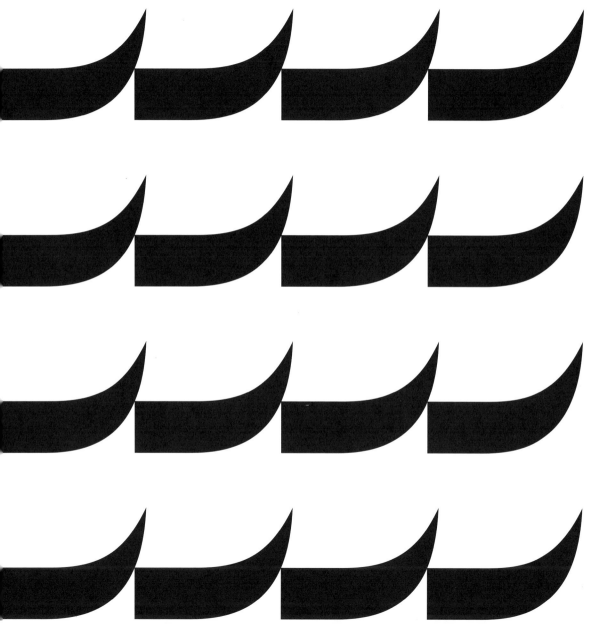

I happen, and then I happen again, and again.

You can go the long distance!

At the end of the day, I also like a rest.

This is me; I'm the semicolon.

;

Semicolon burning bright
In the forests of the night;
What immortal hand or eye
Could frame my fearful asymmetry?

Records show I was first spotted in 1644;
I've been on the prowl for closely related
ideas ever since.

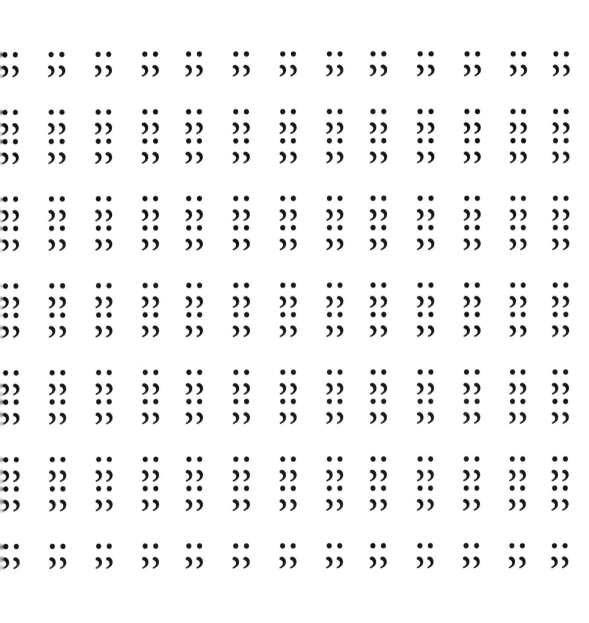

Prized for my grace,
though close to extinction,
I have a tail with a tip
and taste of distinction.

I am nimble; I am beautiful.

I live in disguise though am always there;
I am half of earth, half of air.

People don't think they need me; they do.

This is me, colon: and on and on.

I am the dots of:
elaboration,
affirmation,
confirmation,
celebration,
continuation,
recitation,
observation,
enumeration,
information,
proclamation,
reverberation,
revelation.

I help in the progress of things.

Life's all about the gaps between.

That's me, apostrophe.

I was once known as the 'mark of laziness.'

ose

TBH, I do like cutting corners.

And I'll own up: I'm a bit possessive.

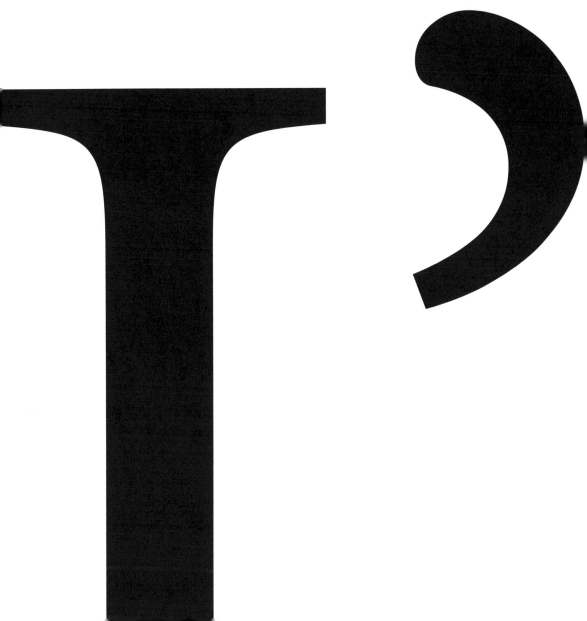

People get possessive about me, too.
There's even an Apostrophe Protection
Society in Britain.

I love to love and be loved. Autograph?
Of course.

I say, better to use me than not at all.

asparagu's

(This is us, brackets.)

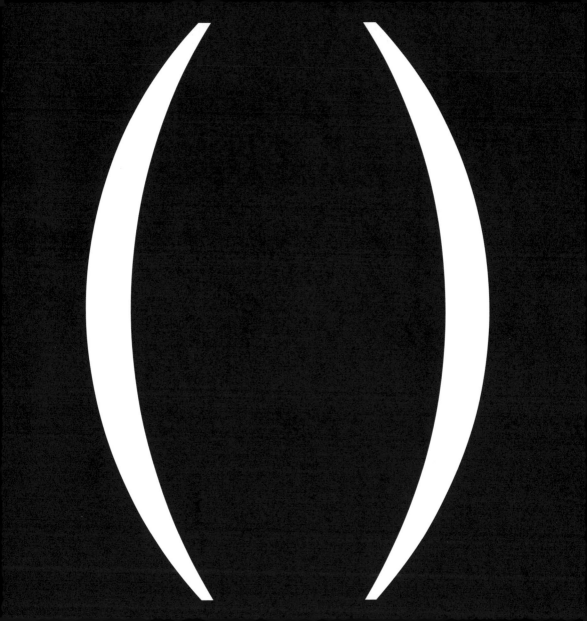

Some say brackets, some say parentheses.

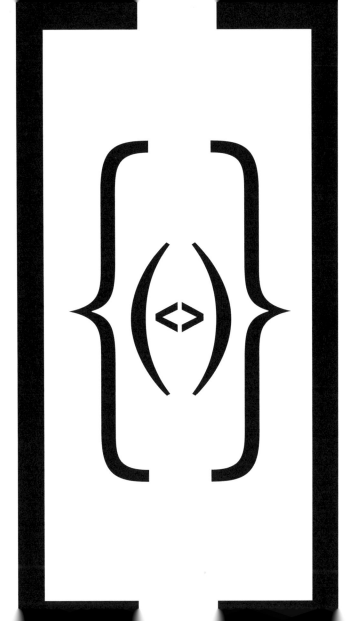

We don't mind what you call us.

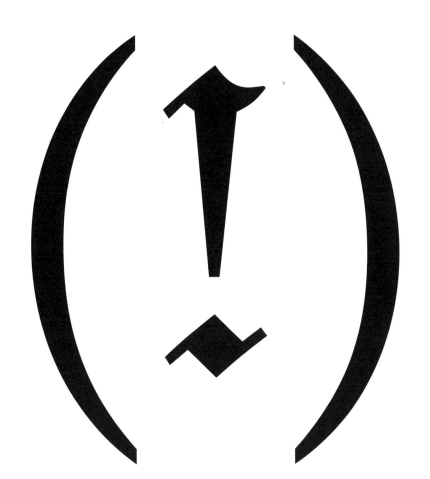

For some reason you only see us from the side.

We do love a bit of gossip.

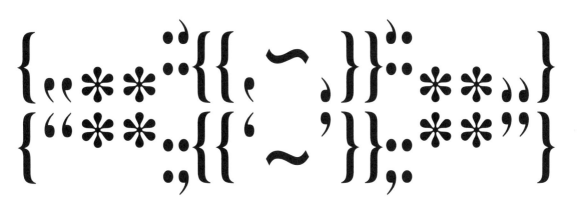

(Between you and me...well, ev

rything's between you and me.)

We need each other (like the day
needs the night).

Once we open something, we always close it.

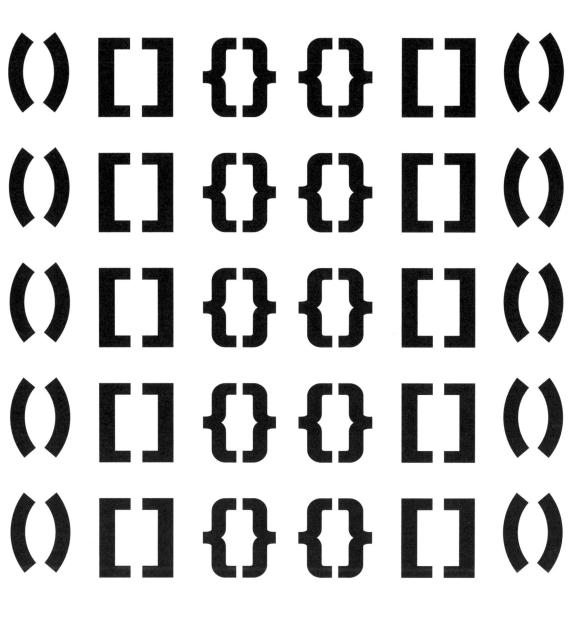

This is me — long dash.

I walk so fast I trip —

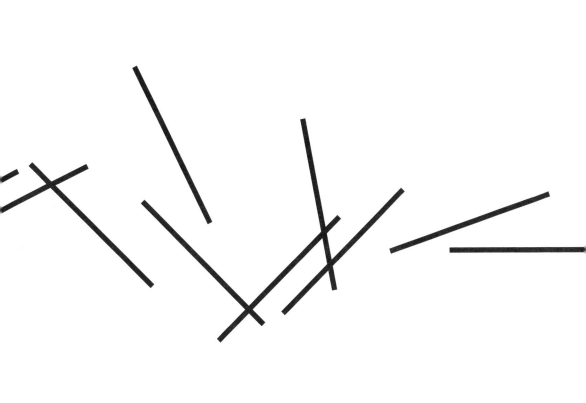

En garde!
I am the swordsr

an of your heart—

Sometimes I — I — I —

Size isn't everything, Monsieur, but I am wider than the hyphen.

I am the mark that sto

elevation   the defia

—

—

ɔs and starts   in my

e of gravitation.

Hi-p

hen!

I disrupt — to move on up.

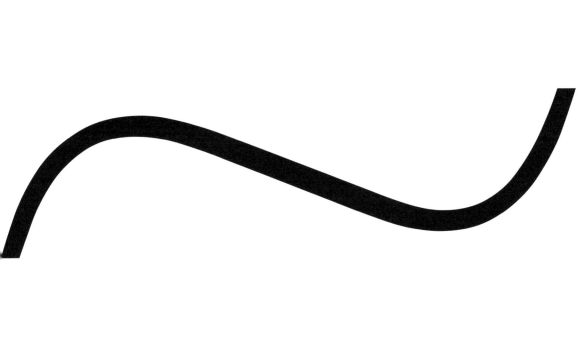

This is us, "quotation marks".

"We love a chat, don't we?"

"It's good to talk but it's even better to listen."

"Sometimes we can't tell what's real and what's not."

"Yeah, there's the truth and then there's '*the truth*'."

"We are the punctuation snark."

"*We are the punctuation snark.*"

"That's what I said."

"I know."

"What's wrong?"

"I feel a bit up in the air."

"What are you thinking of?"

"Guess."

"Um, oh I can't!"

"OK, I'll tell you, but only when they turn the page."

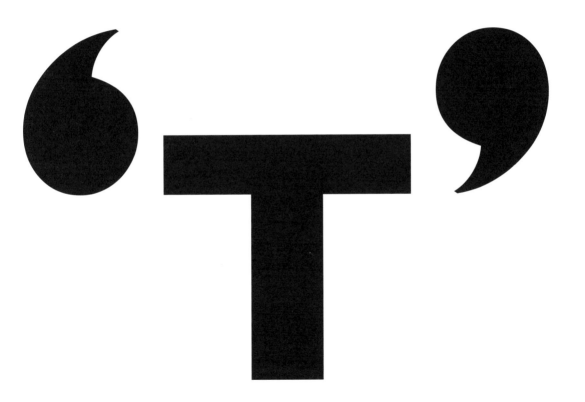

"We're the only punctuation mark your body evolved fingers for."

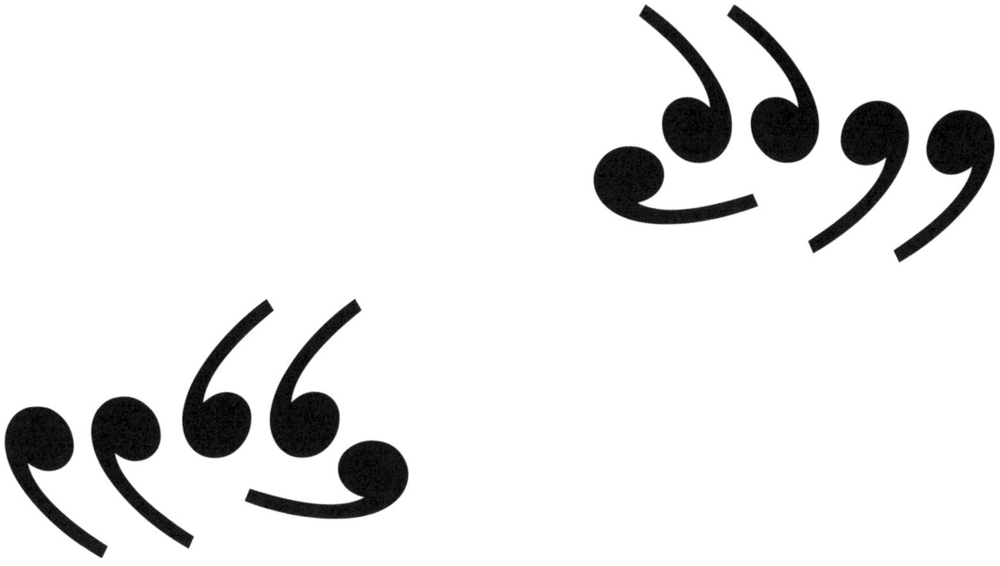

This is me/forward slash.

I sit on the fence/I am both for and against.

I help you cope with this
complicated/wonderful life.

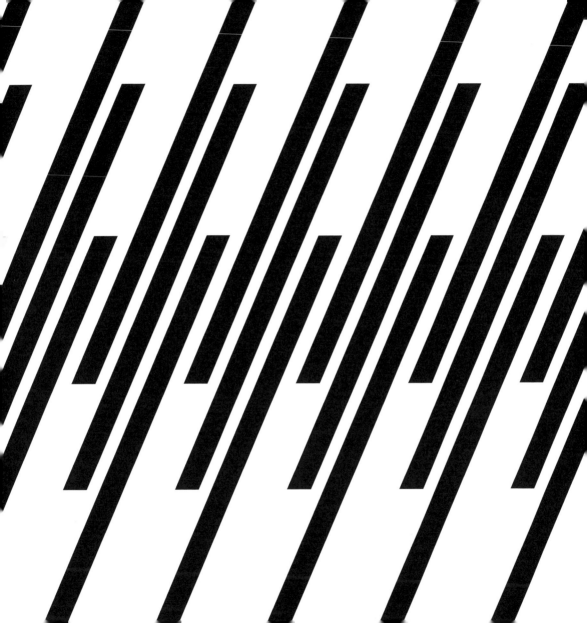

I've thought about it / I never have.

This is me me me, exclamation mark!

I was originally 'the point of admiration'.

As in, I'm crazy about you!

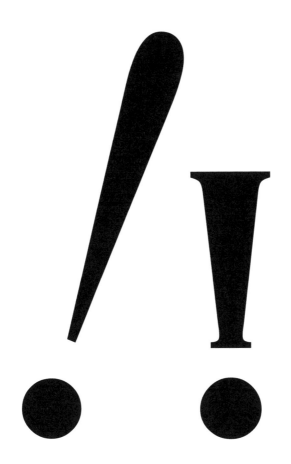

Now I'm the selfie of grammar.

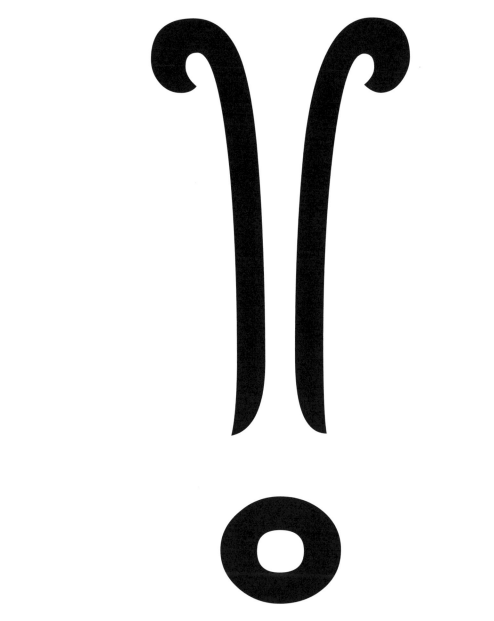

Notice me!

Is this me, question mark?

Some people think, back in the day,
a monk copied the shape of his cat's tail
to make the first ever question mark.

I wonder what gave him that idea?

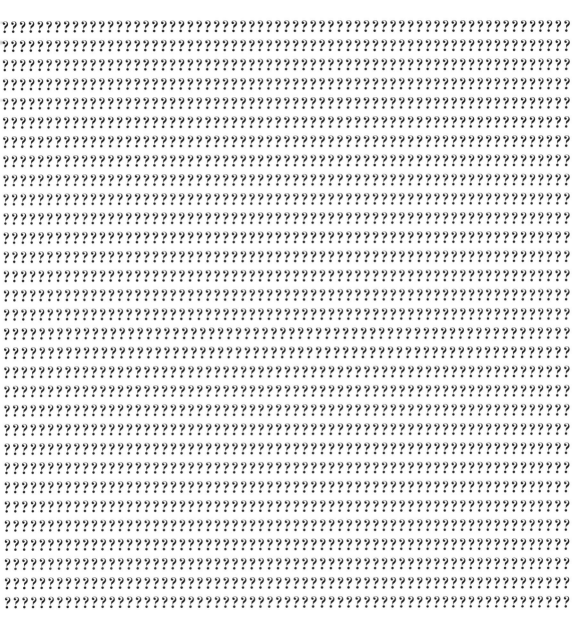

I purr, I pad, I pause...

...I pounce.

Meow.

This is me, ellipsis...

I am the dot dot dots of time passing, the unspoken, the tricky-to-say...

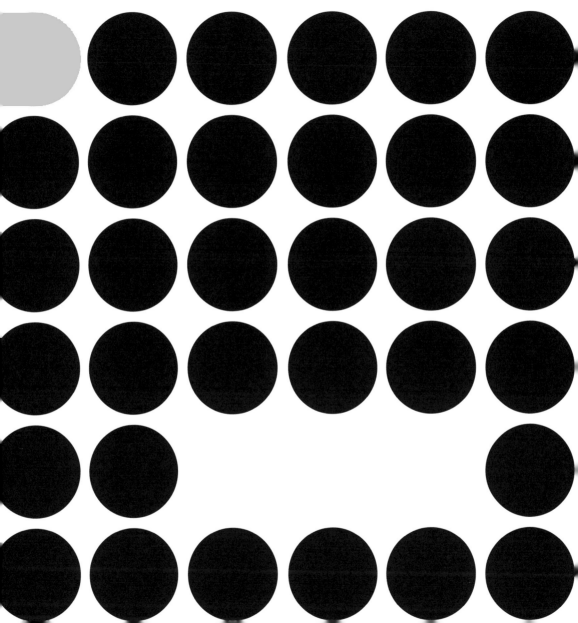

...of scandal, sensation and innuendo...

...of life, the universe and everything...

Typefaces used in this book:

Apple Chancery
Arial Narrow Bold
Arial Black
Avenir Next Condensed
Balega LT
Baskerville
Bauer Bodoni
Bauer Bodoni Bold
Bauer Bodoni Italic
Bell MT
Bell MT Italic
Bella Stencil
Bembo
Bodoni Poster Compressed
Brush Script
Caslon 540
Caslon Pro Italic

Century Schoolbook Italic
Century Schoolbook Roman
Colombine Bold
Copperplate
De Vinne
Didot
DIN Alternate Bold
Engravers Bold
Galliard Italic
Garamond Bold
Gill Sans
Gill Sans Shadowed
Goudy Ornate
Grotesque Black
Grotesque Bold
Johnston Medium
Minion

Modern No 20
Mostra Three Bold
Neutraface 2 Text Book
Neutraface 2 Text Book Italic
Neutraface 2 Text Demi
New Baskerville
Plantin Bold
Raleigh Bold
Sabon
Savoye
Scotch Roman
Snell Roundhand
Times New Roman
Trajan Bold
Trajan Regular
Typeface Six
Wedding Text

Acknowledgements

We would like to thank
Kara Johnson, Sakiko
Kobayashi, Peter Ruane
and Tess Wicksteed at
Here; Helen Conford and
Jim Stoddart at Particular
Books; and Claire Conrad
at Janklow & Nesbit.

Here.

Writer Philip Cowell and
co-founder and Creative
Partner Caz Hildebrand
come from Here, a studio
of thinkers, designers and
makers that work in the
pursuit of creating useful
and beautiful things.

I'm the full stops that cannot fully stop...